Henry James Coleridge, Father Salmeron

The Theology of the Parables

Henry James Coleridge, Father Salmeron

The Theology of the Parables

ISBN/EAN: 9783744797115

Printed in Europe, USA, Canada, Australia, Japan

Cover: Foto ©Lupo / pixelio.de

More available books at **www.hansebooks.com**

The Theology of the Parables.

BY

HENRY JAMES COLERIDGE,

OF THE SOCIETY OF JESUS.

WITH

AN ARRANGEMENT OF THE PARABLES,

In Illustration of the Gospels read in the Mass from Ash Wednesday to Easter Tuesday,

BY FATHER SALMERON.

LONDON:

BURNS, OATES, & CO. 17 PORTMAN STREET,
AND 63 PATERNOSTER ROW.

1877

The Theology of the Parables.

———◦∘◦———

FEW things are more definitely marked off by the sacred historians of the life of our Blessed Lord than the beginning of His teaching by means of parables. It was something which the Apostles did not expect, and as to which they questioned Him at the time. He gave them a distinct and precise answer as to His reason for adopting a new practice in His teaching, which answer has been recorded for our guidance. From this answer, and from an examination of the parables themselves, we may expect to obtain a clue as to any particular characteristics of the teaching in question which furnished the motive for the change of method adopted by our Lord. And we may, at the same time, be able to settle the question which naturally arises concerning the parables—the question, namely, whether they form a distinct body of teaching with reference to a particular subject, or whether the difference between them and the rest of our Lord's instructions was simply one of form.

With regard to this last question, it is pertinent to observe that the parabolic form of teaching was not

now used by our Blessed Lord for the first time,
unless we are disposed to insist very strictly upon
characteristics which may seem almost technical,
such as some direct declaration of our Lord that He
taught by comparison.   When our Blessed Lord said
to Simon the Pharisee, as St. Mary Magdalene was
kneeling at His feet, "A certain man had two
debtors; one owed him five hundred pence and the
other fifty, and when they had nothing to pay he
forgave them both,"* it can hardly be questioned
that He spoke a parable in the common sense of the
word, as much as when He said to the priests and
scribes at Jerusalem—"What think you?   A certain
man had two sons, and going to the first he said,
Son, go to-day and work in my vineyard.   And he
answered, I will not, and afterwards repented and
went.   And going to the other he said likewise.   And
he answered, I go, sir, and went not."†   The two
passages are almost exactly parallel, each terminating
in a question put by our Lord to the person or
persons whom He wished to instruct.   But the first
case took place before the teaching by parables began,
and the last case occurred at the very end of our
Lord's ministry.   In the earlier teaching of our Lord,
we find from the very beginning that use of images

---

* St. Luke vii. 40, seq. ; *Vita Vitæ*, § 55.   The substance of this
Essay has been taken from a Commentary on the author's *Vita Vitæ
Nostræ Meditantibus Proposita* (London : Burns & Oates, 1869), and
the references which are of any service as to questions of Harmony and
the order of the events of our Lord's life have therefore been retained.
For the same reason, the order followed in that work has been assumed
without question throughout.

† St. Matt. xxi. 28—32 ; *Vita Vitæ*, § 135.

and similitudes which is the foundation of the parabolic system. There are certain passages which we
may almost speak of as formal parables, such as the
words about the land already white unto harvest, the
sower and reaper being different and yet rejoicing
together, addressed to the disciples after our Lord's
conversation with the woman at the well of Samaria,*
and more than one part of the Sermons on the Mount
and on the Plain, such as the address to the disciples
as the salt of the earth and the light of the world, the
images of the father giving his children bread and fish
rather than stones or serpents, of the wolves in sheep's
clothing, of the beam and mote in the eye, of the
blind leading the blind, of the trees known by their
fruit, and the almost direct parable at the end of each
of these two sermons of the man who built his house
on the rock and the other man who built his house
upon the sand.†

Passing on a little further in the Gospels, we have
the image of the house divided against itself, and of
the strong armed man whose goods are made spoil
of by a stronger than he.‡ All these passages are
placed at an earlier stage of our Lord's ministry
than the formal commencement of His teaching by
parables, and they make it appear improbable that
the great difference between our Lord's teaching as
addressed to the people before and after that commencement is to be found simply, or even principally,

* St. John iv. 35.
† St. Matt. v. vi. vii. 24—27; St. Luke vi. 20—49; *Vita Vitæ,*
§ 31—36, 47—49.
‡ St. Matt. xii. ; St. Mark iii. ; *Vita Vitæ,* § 56.

in the form which it assumed in its several stages respectively. If a modern teacher, who had up to a certain time been accustomed to direct dogmatic or moral instruction, were suddenly to change his method of procedure, and teach only by fable or allegory what he had before taught in another way, the difference would be described as consisting mainly in the form. If a teacher, who had before very frequently used familiar images and similitudes, or even anecdotes, to inculcate moral truths, were to abandon any other method and throw his similitudes more strictly into the form of parables, such a change might perhaps arrest attention and cause inquiry, but it would hardly claim the great importance which appears to be attached to the change made by our Lord in the present instance.

We are thus prepared for a further inquiry into the answers given by our Blessed Lord to the questions of the Apostles, and into the parables themselves, as far as these may shed light upon the precise nature of this new phase in our Lord's teaching. Our Lord's answer to the question, "Why dost Thou speak unto them in parables?" is placed by St. Matthew immediately after the first parable, that of the Sower and the Seed.* It contains much that is repeated by St. Mark (iv. 10) when he gives the explanation of that first parable, in answer to a question as to its meaning which must not be confounded with the more general question as to the reasons for the parabolic teaching as such. Leaving aside some apparent difficulties of interpretation,

* St. Matt. xiii. 10, seq. ; *Vita Vitæ*, § 59.

with which it is not at present our business to deal, we may state the answer much in this way—" To those to whom I thus speak it is not given, as it is given to you, to know the mystery of the Kingdom of God. For he that hath, to him shall be given, and he shall abound ; but he that hath not, from him shall be taken away that which he hath." The mystery of the Kingdom of God, therefore, is the subject of the parables, and it is in some sense an advance upon and an addition to the knowledge already possessed by the Apostles. " I speak to them in parables," our Blessed Lord continues, " because seeing they do not see, and hearing they do not hear, neither do they understand. And in them is fulfilled the prophecy of Esaias, who saith : With the hearing ye shall hear, and shall not understand, and seeing ye shall see, and shall not perceive. For the heart of this people is grown gross, and with their ears they have been dull of hearing, and their eyes they have shut, lest at any time they should see with their eyes and hear with their ears and understand with their heart, and be converted, and I should heal them." This is the reason given by our Lord for His speaking to the multitude in parables. Their hearts are too hard for the mystery of God's Kingdom. He is acting on His own precept, given in the Sermon on the Mount, about not casting pearls before swine, " lest perhaps they trample them under their feet, and turning upon you they tear you."*

But, on the other hand, the parables contained, to those who could understand them, something ex-

* St. Matt. vii. 6.

ceedingly precious. They were, to use the heathen
poet's words, full of speech to those who could understand them, and the doctrine which they contained
was enshrined in them in that particular form, in
order that "to him that hath" more "might be
given." Thus our Lord continues to His Apostles—
"Blessed are your eyes, because they see, and your
ears, because they hear. For, amen, I say to you,
many prophets and just men have desired to see the
things that you see, and have not seen them, and to
hear the things that you hear, and have not heard
them." And we find Him showing a kind of tender
anxiety for them, lest they should not profit suffi-
ciently by this teaching of "the mystery of the
Kingdom of God." Thus, before expounding the
parable of the Seed, He says, "Are you ignorant of
this parable? and how shall you know all parables?"*
as if they were to contain a body of instruction
given in a definite number of comparisons. And
again, after the explanation, "Take heed what you
hear. In what measure you shall mete it shall be
measured unto you again, and more shall be given
you. For he that hath to him shall be given, and
he that hath not that also which he hath shall be
taken away from him."† All these passages seem to
prepare us for the conclusion that the parables do
not differ merely in form from other instructions of
our Lord to the people, such as the Sermon on the
Mount, and, in part, the Sermon on the Plain, but that
there may be some general subject more particularly
set forth in them, to be instructed concerning which

* St. Mark iv. 13.   † St. Mark iv. 24, 25.

was a great and high privilege, of which careless persons were not worthy, and of which the full revelation had hitherto been reserved by God's providence. It might seem, also, that this knowledge was especially required for those who, like the Apostles, were not only to be the subjects of the new kingdom, but also its ministers and propagators. After the first series of parables, He turned to them and asked, "Have ye understood all these things? They say to Him, Yes. He said unto them, Therefore every scribe instructed in the Kingdom of Heaven is like to a man that is a householder, who bringeth forth out of his treasure new things and old."*

What, then, is this head or subject of divine teaching and knowledge which is set forth so specially in the parables, if we are to consider them as differing from former teaching of our Lord not only in form, but, to a certain extent, in subject and scope? If we consider the moral or practical truths which are undoubtedly conveyed in the parables, we may well be disposed to class them under different heads, and to find a great variety of subjects treated of in them. A recent author, whose work,† though cast in a very simple and popular form, shows much study and thoughtfulness, has thus classed the parables under four heads:— 1. Parables concerning the Church. 2. Parables concerning God's dealings with us. 3. Parables concerning our conduct to God. 4. Parables concerning our conduct to other men. Such divisions are of much practical use; but they

---

* St. Matt. xiii. 51, 52.

† The *New Testament Narrative, &c.* Burns & Oates, 1868.

are to a great extent arbitrary. In the work to which we allude, for instance, the parables of the Friend at Midnight and the Unjust Judge fall under the third head—parables concerning our conduct to God ; and that of the Good Samaritan under the head of our conduct to other men. But the two former are most certainly meant to encourage us to prayer by setting forth God's way of yielding to it under two images of successful importunity, and that of the Good Samaritan must with equal certainty be assigned to the class of those which set forth God's dealings with us in the work of our redemption after the Fall, and this charity of God to us is made the pattern of our charity to others. We need not discuss other methods of division which may have been suggested, and which have very often much practical usefulness to recommend them. A very interesting arrangement of the parables will be found in the last chapter (ch. xlii.) of Salmeron's volume of Commentary on them—the seventh volume of his great work. In this arrangement the parables are adapted to the Gospels for the several days of Lent, in order, from Ash Wednesday up to Easter Tuesday, and the adaptation will be found to suggest many striking reflections. It is, however, as an adaptation, not as a systematic arrangement, that we mention it here.

We believe that it will be found easier to grasp the main idea of the parables as a whole, if we consider that they are meant to illustrate one great head of doctrine which is most naturally fitted for promulgation under this particular form. The parables differ, of course, from the other teaching of our Lord in their descriptive character, the lesson being left to be gathered from the truths involved in the description. And that which is the subject of description, that one great head to which the parables refer, is that which forms only one of the heads in the division lately mentioned—that is, God in His dealings with His creatures, and especially man. Before proceeding to the actual proof of this, with reference to the parables, we may say a few words on the degree to which, if we may be allowed the expression, the thought of the government of the world by God seems to have drawn to itself the tenderest devotion and most constant attention of the Sacred Heart of the Incarnate Son.

It is said of Him in the very outset of the Gospel history, " The law was given by Moses, but grace and truth came by Jesus Christ." Moses gave a rule of action, Jesus Christ brought grace to enable men to keep the law of God ; but He brought not only grace, but truth, knowledge which had not been before given concerning His Father—" God no man hath ever seen, the only-begotten Son, Who is in the bosom of the Father, He hath declared Him."* The English word " declare," in its present sense, is but a poor substitute for the full meaning of the Greek, or of the Latin word by which the Vulgate has rendered the Greek. St. John seems to mean a full and perfect revelation, as far as such revelation is possible to our capacities. At the very end of His last most intimate discourse to His Apostles, our Lord spoke of the

---

* St. John i. 18. The Greek word is ἐξηγήσατο. The Latin is *enarravit.*

same subject as the great matter of His instructions. "The hour cometh when I shall no longer speak to you in proverbs, but shall tell you openly of the Father.*" It is well known that St. John throughout uses the word which is rendered "proverbs" in the same sense as the "parables" of the other Evangelists. From the first recorded words of our Lord down to the last, from the speech to our Blessed Lady in the Temple, "How is it that ye sought Me, did ye not know that I must be about My Father's business?" to the cry on the Cross in which He breathed out His Soul, "Father, into Thy hands I commend My spirit," we can find very few utterances of our Lord which do not directly or indirectly refer to His Father. The particular subject of which we are speaking—that is, the providential dealings of God with men and with His creatures—is characteristically prominent in the earlier teaching of our Lord. To some extent it was less directly mentioned as time went on and as opposition grew.

We may illustrate what we mean by a comparison of the two great discourses, the Sermon on the Mount and the Sermon on the Plain. They were delivered perhaps, at no very great interval of time. The choice of the twelve Apostles, which was immediately followed by the delivery of the second sermon, may probably have taken place about the Pentecost after the second Passover of our Lord's ministry; and the Sermon on the Mount, the first of the two, may have been delivered late in the first year. But between the two had sprung up the first formal and organized

* St. John xvi. 25.

opposition to our Lord on the part of the Jewish authorities, first at Jerusalem, and afterwards in Galilee, on account of what they deemed His laxity about the Sabbath-day, on which day He had healed the impotent man at the Pool, defended the disciples for plucking the ears of corn, and worked a second miracle—perhaps after His return from Jerusalem to Galilee—on the man with the withered hand in the synagogue.* It was after this that our Lord began to withdraw Himself from His enemies, in a manner which St. Matthew has specially mentioned as one of the chain of fulfilments of prophecy to which he draws attention all through his Gospel.† We need not draw out the similarity or the differences which mark the two Sermons further than is useful for our present purpose ; but there is in the second a marked absence of that free loving mention of God as our Father which characterizes the Sermon on the Mount. Most of the beatitudes are wanting in the later discourse ; as also the injunction to " let your light shine before men, that they may see your good works and glorify your Father Who is in heaven." The very words "your Father" occur only once in the Sermon on the Plain, and then in a passage parallel to a part of the Sermon on the Mount, in which the reference to God's dealings is expanded by a twofold and beautiful illustration. In St. Luke it is only, " Love ye your enemies, do good, and lend, hoping

* St. John v. ; St. Matt. xii. 1—8 ; St. Mark ii. 23—28 ; St. Luke vi. 1—5 ; and St. Matt. xii. 9—14 ; St. Mark iii. 1—6 ; St. Luke vi. 6—11. *Vita Vitæ,* § 41—44.

† St. Matt. xii. 17—19.

for nothing thereby, and your reward shall be great,
and you shall be the sons of the Highest, for He is
kind to the unthankful and to the evil."*   In the
Sermon on the Mount the image is far more definite.
"I say to you, Love your enemies, do good to them
that hate you, and pray for them that persecute and
calumniate you, that you may be the children of
your Father Who is in heaven, Who maketh His sun
to rise upon the good and bad, and raineth upon the
just and the unjust."†   In the part of the Sermon on
the Mount which follows, the mention of "your
Father in heaven" meets us in almost every verse.
Almsgiving is to be done in secret, that our Father
Who seeth in secret may repay it.   Prayer is to
be made in secret, for the same reason.   The "Our
Father" is given in full, but it is omitted in the
Sermon on the Plain, and the petition about forgiveness is explained by reference to the rules by which
our Father will be guided in dealing with us.   Then
follow precepts about fasting, the motive of which is
the same reference to the Father.   Then there are
passages about not serving two masters, about absolute confidence in our Father, Who knoweth all our
needs, Who feeds the birds of the air, and clothes the
lilies of the field, and about expecting an answer to
prayer, because our Father will certainly give good
things to those who ask Him more readily than any
earthly father to his own children.   In fact, in men-
tioning the passages of this kind which are to be
found in the first Sermon, and which are omitted in
the second, we have gone a good way towards a

* St. Luke vi. 35.   † St. Matt. v. 44, 45.

perfect enumeration of the differences between the two discourses.* We are far from saying that no other reason than that which is here suggested occasioned these differences, for the audience to which the Sermon on the Plain was addressed, seems to have been made up of a mixed crowd, among whom there may even have been some heathen, and the Sermon on the Mount was delivered to those who were more nearly followers of our Lord. But we think that there is good reason for maintaining that the progress of opposition had much to do with the more reserved character of our Lord's teaching at the later period of the two.

But after the Sermon on the Plain had been delivered, a further development of the malignant opposition to our Lord had taken place, very different in character from the captious objection made against Him from the letter of the law about the Sabbathday. His enemies now took the line of attributing His miracles to a compact with Beelzebub; thus making themselves guilty of the blasphemy against the Holy Ghost, and imputing to Satan that very providential agency of love and mercy which was

---

* We may add another illustration, which may at first sight seem to refer to a merely accidental difference. On the first occasion when our Lord cast the buyers and sellers out of the Temple, St. John tells us that He said to them who sold doves, "Take these things away, and make not *the house of my Father* a house of traffic" (St. John ii. 16). On the second occasion, after Palm Sunday, and therefore at the end of His teaching, He is described by the other three Evangelists as saying more formally, "It is written, My house shall be called a house of prayer, but you have made it a den of thieves" (St. Matt. xxi. 13; St. Luke xix. 46). St. Mark's words are slightly different (xi. 17).

designed by God to be the remedy for mankind through the Incarnation. We know our Lord's indignation at this charge, and the very strong language He used concerning it. It is from this time that we have to date His denunciations of that evil generation, of which the latter state was to be made worse than the first. And it is from this time also that we are to date the beginning to teach by parables.

There is certainly abundant ground for considering that our Blessed Lord, to speak of Him after a human manner, felt Himself full of knowledge concerning God and His ways with His creatures, which He burned to impart to those to whom He was sent, but which they were not fit to receive. At the outset of His history we have an account of His conversation with Nicodemus,* to whom He spoke about the necessity of a new birth in Baptism with a plainness and openness which are surprising to us when we compare them with many parts of His subsequent teaching. There is the same directness of instruction to be remarked in the conversation which follows, in St. John, between our Lord and the woman of Samaria. When He said to her about the Messias, " I Who speak unto thee am He,"† He made a direct assertion which He made at no other time, except when adjured by Caiaphas to declare whether He were the Christ, the Son of the Blessed. But to Nicodemus He used words of complaint, as if He were surprised at the dulness of his perception of spiritual truth—" Amen, amen, I say to thee, that we speak what we know and we testify what we have

---

* St. John iii. 1, seq.   † *Ibid.* iv. 26.

seen, and you receive not our testimony. I have spoken unto you earthly things, and you believe not, how will you believe if I shall speak unto you heavenly things ? "* We need not draw out here the whole that might be said concerning this difficulty, which our Lord experienced almost universally and to the very end of His ministry, in meeting with hearts and minds capable of receiving His divine doctrine. But these considerations prepare us to find that, when the time had come for Him to teach the people more fully about God, and especially about that great revelation of Himself which is contained in His providence and in the arrangement of His kingdom, in the widest sense of that word, He found Himself constrained to adopt this particular mode of teaching more exclusively, by means of which the mystery of the Kingdom might be enshrined in the most familiar form, a form which can hardly escape the memory after that faculty has once taken it in, and yet be so enshrined therein as not to be thrust upon the notice of those incapable of understanding it, while at the same time it invited the thoughtful pondering of those whose hearts were already to some extent enlightened concerning it. If we might be so bold as to compare what passed in our Lord's Sacred Heart with what is noblest and best in the workings and productions of the most gifted of men—

> "Those whose hearts are beating high
> With the pulse of poesy"—

we may venture to say that He was fain to pour

* St. John iii. 11, 12.

forth, in some form analogous to the highest song, the thoughts to which the possession of all the knowledge concerning God with which the Sacred Humanity was endowed gave birth.   The knowledge thus given to Him, like the other graces and treasures which He received at the time of the Hypostatic Union, were given, not for Himself alone, but for us— for the children of the Church throughout all ages ; and we may consider those instructions of His, which the providence of His Father had determined should come down to us in the Gospel narratives, as having been framed for us as well as for those to whom they were immediately addressed.   The revelation of the Father, which it was His commission to make to mankind, was thus made independent of the unworthiness and dulness and hardness of heart of those by whom He happened to be immediately surrounded during so large a portion of His teaching. If we are to apply to the Sacred Heart the rule which our Lord Himself gave, and say that out of the abundance of the heart the mouth speaketh, so that we may judge of His habitual thoughts by the subjects that are always upon His lips, we must certainly say that the character and perfections of the Father were ever His darling subjects of contemplation.   When the heart that was most near and most like unto His own, the heart of His Blessed Mother, poured itself out in her holy canticle of thanksgiving, it was a strain that spoke of one wonderful perfection of God after another—His Lordship, His Providence in Redemption, His Condescension to the humble, His Power, His Sanctity, His Mercy, His Faithfulness in His promises, and that law of His Kingdom whereby the proud are confounded, the lowly exalted, the hungry filled, and the rich sent empty away. We cannot, then, be far wrong if we venture to approach the parables of our Lord with this thought in our minds—that they contain more, perhaps, than any other part of His teaching, His description of His Father in His dealings with those who belong to Him. Let us allow ourselves to suppose that to these applies, at least as fully as to any other of His discourses, the text already quoted from St. John—" The only-begotten Son, Who is in the bosom of the Father, He hath declared Him."

We shall perhaps find that this view of the parables will bring their signification more into a harmonious whole than any other, and that, on the other hand, we hardly require a more complete system of teaching as to God and His providence than that which is here contained. No doubt, a number of them refer immediately to the Church ; but the Church is one great manifestation or fruit of God's Fatherly Love, and the laws on which He has acted in respect to the Church have not been confined in their operation to what immediately concerns her. No doubt the far greater number of them, again, are meant to convey some distinct moral or practical lesson, such as the necessity of vigilance, or of Christian prudence, or the law of charity or of mutual forgiveness of injuries; but these lessons are pointed in the parables by distinct reference to something in God's character or ways of dealing with us, which is the more immediate subject of the picture. And, perhaps, it may also be found—and this is the last argument for which there is room in the present paper—that this particular view of the general scope of the teaching by parables may explain some features in them which are otherwise the occasion of difficulties more or less serious. Nor would it materially interfere with this view as to the general purport of the teaching by parables, if we find that our Lord now and then used the same form with another object, such as we can hardly help seeing, for instance, in the parable of the Two Sons,* which He Himself explained as applying to the conduct of the priests and scribes on the one hand, and of the publicans and harlots on the other, with respect to the baptism of St. John. Nor, again, must it be urged against us that some of the parables, as that of the Labourers in the Vineyard, and the Unmerciful Servant, are undoubtedly addressed to the most intimate followers of our Lord. All these parables speak of great laws of God's Kingdom—and this is the main point on which we insist.

When we consider Who God is, and how infinitely His attributes and nature are above our comprehension, it must be obvious at once that His government of the universe must be, as a whole and in its parts, very far above the ken of our mental faculties, though at the same time it is equally true that in nature and in providence, as well as in the supernatural order, He distinctly reveals Himself, and intends us to learn about Him from His works and ways. He is the one great object of the study and contemplation of all

* St. Matt. xxi. 26—32.

created intelligent beings, and at the same time He must, as it were, break the knowledge of Himself to us tenderly, He must raise us on high and add fresh power to our eyes before we can gaze on Him. If we could fully understand Him and His ways, He would not be our God ; if we could know nothing about Him and about them, we should not be the creatures He has made us, and our life here would not be a preparation for the blessedness which He intends for us hereafter, and of which we even now enjoy the ·partial foretaste. The very first thing that we know about Him is a mystery to us, in the common sense of the word. For the first great mystery in the providence of God—in which we may include the creation as well as the government of the world—is that permission and tolerance of evil which follows as a necessary consequence from the planting of free creatures in a state of probation. Let us never underrate this. It has its answer, but not all can see it. Those familiar with the difficulties which practically beset and bewilder no inconsiderable number even of Christian and Catholic souls to whom the world is a puzzle and a riddle, will hardly question the importance of this difficulty, which pushes itself, if we may so say, in so many different directions, making men at one time question the justice of the decree which has loaded them with the responsibility of a choice whose issue is eternal, at another time doubt of the love which can create beings whom it foreknows shall be everlastingly miserable, or again, at another, rise up against the sentence which visits the rebellion of a weak and sorely tempted creature with a punishment so great as that which awaits the wicked in the next world. Or again, the difficulty takes the form, as we see in some of the Psalms, to quote no other example, of an inability to understand the prosperity of vice, the apparent impunity in this life of the enemies of God, and the afflictions and calamities which befall the just. Or, again, the thing which is unintelligible seems to be that God's work is so much marred and fettered in the world, that there is so little result for so great an expenditure of love, labour, and sacrifice, and that mischief is allowed to flourish even in the very home of good, and to corrupt those who would otherwise serve God in innocence and faithfulness. All these difficulties have, then, their answer in the knowledge of God and of His character, His attributes, and His ways with men, and most of them are touched by the remark of St. Augustine, that God chooses rather to bring good out of evil than not to permit evil. Others, again, are met as St. Paul usually, in the first instance, meets difficulties about providence and predestination, by a consideration of the absolute lordship and dominion of God over His creatures, whom He may place under whatever conditions He will, consistently, as whatever He wills must be consistent, with His justice and His holiness. And after this consideration of the absolute authority and ownership—so to speak—of a Creator over His creatures, there naturally follow others which are required also for difficulties of another kind, as well as for those of which we have spoken—considerations of God's immense and boundless goodness, His tender care over His own, His mercy and long-suffering and indulgence to those who oppose themselves to Him, His ever-ready grace, His fatherly attention to prayer, and the like. Another great head of what we may call in general the mystery of God's government contains the whole chain of His dealings with man in respect of his fall and redemption, the arrangements made for his recovery, the manner in which it is brought about, and the special laws of the new kingdom which is its organ, and through which its blessings are administered. Here we come to what in a more restricted sense may be considered as the " mystery" of God's Kingdom—the Divine "economy" of grace which is worked out through the Incarnation by means of an exquisite system, full of beauty, gentleness, and tenderness, the principles and many of the details of which will be found, on close inspection, to be figured in the parables. All these things are what they are in detail on account of something which may be known and reflected on concerning God, and they cannot be understood and valued unless with respect to Him, and as reflecting His goodness or holiness, or mercifulness or justice.

This is a very imperfect as well as a very general description of the sort of truths which may be conceived as forming the more substantial points in the teaching by parables—the points to which other things are subordinated, and with reference to which those other things are best to be understood. The first of all the formal parables, which is also one of those few parables which our Lord Himself has explained in detail, seems at first sight to be a description of the different ways in which the word of God—in whatever form and under whatever dispensation—is received by man. But it is commonly called the parable of the Sower,* from its first words and from its principal figure, God, Who sows His seed broadcast and with so much profusion, and seems; as has so often been remarked, in both His material and His spiritual creation, to waste so many beginnings which do not come to maturity, for the sake, if we may so speak, of the rich and multiplied beauty and fruitfulness of a few. This law, which runs through the whole of God's kingdom, as far as we know it, suggests many truths concerning Him— His magnificence and liberality, the manner in which even imperfect works, as they seem to us, manifest His glory, the dignity which His grace gives to those who co-operate with it, and the like ; while it has a clearer significance when seen working on creations of free beings, who can co-operate with that grace or not, and furnishes a silent commentary on that failure of our Lord's own particular mission of which He had lately been so mournfully complaining. The minute details of the parable, giving so vivid a picture that we almost seem to see the spot on the seashore from which every feature of the image may have been taken, are explained by our Lord of the different circumstances under which so much of the good seed of the Word of God is wasted, while only a part of it takes root in good ground ; and the careful mention of every several cause of failure reminds us of the particular and deliberate manner in which He more

* St. Matt. xiii.; St. Mark iv. ; St. Luke viii.

than once enumerated the successive stages of His own future Passion.* The next parable, known as that of the Tares or Cockle,† tells us still more about the mystery of the kingdom, for in this not only is the good seed wasted, but bad seed is actually sown, and springs up by the side of the good that is not wasted. How many of the difficulties as to God's providence may not be solved by the simple words, "Suffer both to grow until the harvest"? And when we consider that in the spiritual kingdom of God that is possible which is contrary to the laws of the natural kingdom—that the cockle or tare may become the wheat, and the wheat may degenerate into the cockle —we have a fresh revelation of God's tender, and, to use the Scriptural expression, reverential way of dealing with us in the words, "Lest perhaps gathering up the cockle, ye root up the wheat also together with it."

The six parables—those of the Seed that grows secretly, of the Grain of Mustard-seed, of the Leaven, of the Hidden Treasure, the Precious Pearl, and the Draw-net—which follow those of the Sower and of the Tares, may be considered as completing, each by the addition of some special feature, the picture drawn by our Lord in His general dealings in His kingdom.

---

* This prophecy grows in distinctness from the date of the Confession of St. Peter, when it was first made, to that of the last approach to Jerusalem before Palm Sunday. Comp. St. Matt. xvi. 21, St. Mark viii. 31, St. Luke xi. 21 (*Vita Vitæ*, § 82), with St. Matt. xvii. 21, 22, St. Mark ix. 30, St. Luke ix. 44 (*Vita Vitæ*, § 84 ad fin.) ; and again with St. Matt. xx. 18, 19, St. Mark x. 33, 34, St. Luke xviii. 32, 33 (*Vita Vitæ*, § 128).

† St. Matt. xiii. 24—30, 36—53.

God addresses Himself to His creatures, and allows them to refuse or accept Him. He tolerates His enemies until the harvest, for their sake and for the sake of those among whom they live. We have now to see certain characteristics of the work which He carries on in those who receive Him. The parable (given by St. Mark* alone) of the Seed that grows gradually, seems to picture that progress from one virtue to another which is the mark of those who belong to Him, and which accounts for the abundant thirty-fold, sixty-fold, and one hundred-fold, of which mention has been made before. But God works in a double way, by His external word and outward means of grace, and again by the inherent fertility which He imparts to good souls, and the secret influence of His own perpetual action upon each soul in particular. The earth seems to bring forth of itself after the seed has once been implanted, and the result is partly the work of the seed, partly that of the earth. The image of the grain of mustard-seed † seems to represent the outward development and magnificent growth of the work of God in the world, while that of the leaven ‡ explains the law of its growth, which is from within, by the silent spread of the influence of grace, and the assimilation of those natural elements in the mass in which it works which are congenial to it. It need not be questioned that these parables, like many others, are historical and prophetical. But they come true in history, because they represent the principles on which God works,

* St. Mark iv. 26—34 ; *Vita Vitæ*, § 60.
† St. Matt. xiii. 31, 32 ; St. Mark iv. 30—32.
‡ St. Matt. xiii. 33.

and these principles are ultimately the echoes and reflections of His character, His wisdom, His patience, His winning ways with His creatures—that sweetness with whch He "ordereth all things" of which the Scripture speaks.*

The parables of the Treasure hid in a Field, and of the Pearl of Great Price,† which come next in order, are frequently interpreted as if the principal reference were not to God but to those who seek or who find Him and His grace. This interpretation might seem at first sight to be at variance with the view which is set forth in this paper, that the dealings of God with man form the direct subject of the teaching by parables, rather than the dealings of man with God. It must be remembered, however, that no one can truly find or truly seek God without God Himself, and that, as in the reality figured by the parables which have just been mentioned, it is God Who gives to the earth or to the seed its fruitfulness, God Who gives to the hidden leaven its power of spreading and assimilating and penetrating that which it leavens, it is God Who gives to the mustard-seed the power to grow into a great tree, God Who assists in all these cases the development and the exercise of the powers which He has originally created and bestowed—so here in the parables of the Pearl and of the Treasure the holy instinct which seeks the pearl comes from Him, and the seeming accident of finding the treasure comes from Him, as well as the grace by which he that finds either pearl or treasure understands its value, and has the courage

---

* Wisdom viii. 1.   † St. Matt. xiii. 44—46

and prudence to sell all that he has and give it for what he has found. This is a sufficient answer to the objection. But, in truth, there is another interpretation of these two parables, quite as ancient and quite as authoritative as that which has now been explained, and this interpretation applies them directly to God, Who seeks or finds human nature, the human soul, the Church, the great body of His elect, and gives Himself and all that He has in the Incarnation to make the treasure or the pearl His own. This interpretation, we may venture to say, is certainly more in keeping with the Patristic methods of understanding Scripture than the former, though it is far less in harmony with modern ideas, especially among the best Protestants, to whom the moral and more practical interpretation is apparently the only valuable interpretation. We are very far from saying that the one commentary excludes the other. The one may be founded on the other. The primary meaning of the parables may be to represent the action of God in seeking us, the one great ineffable inexplicable outpouring of love of which Creation is the first fruit, Preservation, Providence, Redemption, Sanctification, and Glorification in the possession of God by the Beatific Vision for ever, the final crown ; and the sense which speaks to us of the return of the tide of love from our small and miserable hearts towards God, a return set in motion and guided and maintained by Himself, may be not only true, though secondary, but absolutely involved and founded on and a part of the first.

There remains but one of the first glorious constellation of parables, so to speak ; that in which the

Kingdom of God is compared to a net cast into the sea, which gathers fish of every kind, good and bad.* This is commonly understood of the Church, and the argument drawn from it against the maintainers of an invisible Church composed only of good people is irresistible. But, in the view which is now being discussed, the parable has a still wider meaning, and it comes in at the end of the first series of parables as answering to and in a certain sense balancing the parable of the Sower, which stands in the first place. For in that first parable we have the image of God scattering His seed at random, as it appears, and submitting to the loss of a great part of it for the sake of the return brought in by that which takes root in good soil. In the parable of the Draw-net we see that God acts thus for His own purposes, and brings both good and bad within the range of His action, in order that in the end He may select His own and reject those who are not to be His. When men cast a net into the sea, take into it whatever fish it chances to envelope, and then choose what they will have, and cast the rest away, they exercise that absolute dominion over the lower creatures which God has given them. They may be guilty of cruelty or of some other fault in their conduct to these lower creatures, but they are not guilty of injustice to them, for the lower creatures have no rights in the presence of man. So in God's dealings with us, He must always act according to the ineffable holiness of His own nature, but He is our absolute Master and Lord, as St. Paul more than once argues. We know that He is just to all, and that good and bad fishes in His

* St. Matt. xiii. 47—50.

draw-net are good or bad by virtue of their own will,
according to the measure of their co-operation with
His grace or their resistance to it. But the whole
series of His dealings is for His own sake, that He
may have at the end those who are His elect, and
discard the rest. Thus at the beginning of this
series of parables, God is represented as freely offer-
ing His grace to men who in various ways reject
the good seed; and now at the end of the series, the
other side of the truth is put forward, and it is God
who rejects, and even punishes; for no one is rejected
by Him save through fault of his own. And this
may serve to remind us of the manner in which the
Apostles so frequently speak of the "purpose," the
"good purpose," the "choice" of God, as the source and
root of all Christian blessings on those who have them,
not excluding the action of human free will in the
matter, nor, on the other hand, the desire of God
that all men should be saved, which involves their
having from Him all opportunities of salvation. And
it is to be observed, that when our Lord gives this
parable, He adds an explanation of this part of it
unasked, and that explanation reaches much further
than the words in the parable itself: "So shall it be
at the end of the world. The angels shall go out,
and shall separate the wicked from among the just,
and shall cast them into the furnace of fire; there
shall be weeping and gnashing of teeth."* The
selection to be made at the end of all things, the
reward of the just and the punishment of the wicked,

* St. Matt. xiii. 49, 50.

seem to be the points of the parable on which He particularly insists.

After the grand series of parables on which we have been commenting, we find no more of the same kind of teaching for a very considerable interval in the Gospel history. But St. Mark adds at the end of his account of these, that " with many such parables He spoke to them the word, according as they were able to hear, but without parables He did not speak unto them, but apart He explained all things to His disciples " (iv. 33, 34). The next formal parable, which, as we have said already, is subsequent to these by a long interval, is addressed to His own disciples, in answer to St. Peter's question about forgiving his brother seven times or more.* It comes immediately after His answer to the question, who was greater in the kingdom of heaven, which was also, therefore, a subject of private teaching to His immediate disciples. The moral of the parable of the Unmerciful Servant is of course obvious enough ; but it should be particularly remembered that here again it is the character and way of dealing of God that is the chief and direct subject. The reason why St. Peter, in his suggestion that seven times might be enough to forgive a brother, fell so far short of the mind of our Lord, is to be found in forgetfulness of our position towards God as servants who have to give an account to our Master, Who deals with us as we deal with others, Who has promised to forgive us as we forgive others, and Who has even taught us to pray that our own mercifulness towards others may

---

* St. Matt. xviii. 21—35; *Vita Vitæ*, § 88.

be the measure of His mercifulness towards us.   We
are inclined to stand on our own rights, and measure
the offence against justice which has been committed
by those who injure us ; but the thought of God and
of our debts to Him, and of His dealings towards us
in respect of our faults, raises the question into a
higher sphere altogether.   And here, again, our Lord
goes beyond the immediate necessity of the question
in His answer, which, moreover, He enforces at the
end in words which show that the central truth of
the parable in His mind is the law of God's action
towards us—the most absolute mercifulness and the
most severe reprobation of want of mercy.   " So
also shall My Heavenly Father do to you, if you
forgive not every one his brother from your hearts."

After this new feature, as we may say, added to
our knowledge of God by the parable of the Unmerciful Servant, we pass on to a number of parables
spoken by our Lord in that late period of His
ministry which was mainly spent in Judæa, after His
leaving Galilee in the last of His three years.   A
great number of incidents and discourses in this part
of His life, which is chronicled for us almost exclusively by St. Luke, and which fills up a large portion
of the third Gospel, are repetitions more or less close
of what had been said or done at an earlier period
of His teaching—when He had confined Himself in
the main to Galilee.   We need not pause at present
to point out how natural this is, nor how it solves
completely a great number of the difficulties which
have sometimes perplexed harmonists, sometimes
been made use of by those who would deny the literal

accuracy of the various Gospel narratives. This cycle of parables, so to call it, contains a large proportion of the most famous and well-known of all of them. It is immediately preceded by the discourse recorded by St. John in his tenth chapter as having been delivered at Jerusalem itself after the miracle on the man who had been born blind. In this discourse, although not exactly in form a parable, our Lord sets Himself before us as the Good Shepherd Who giveth His life for the sheep. The series of parables of which we are now speaking begins with that of the Good Samaritan (St. Luke x.), and it embraces that of the Friend roused at midnight (ch. xi.), the Rich Fool (ch. xii.), the discourse about vigilance, in which the figures of the watchful and negligent servants are introduced (*ib.*), the parable again of the Unfruitful Fig-tree (ch. xiii.), the repetition of the parable of the Grain of Mustard-seed (*ib.*), that of the Narrow Gate (*ib.*), that of the guest taking the lowest place (ch. xiv.), of the Great Supper (*ib.*)—which is here given without the addition of the guest without the wedding garment—of the Lost Sheep, the lost piece of money, the Prodigal Son (ch. xv.), the Unjust Steward, the Rich Man and Lazarus (ch. xvi.), the Unjust Judge, and the Publican and the Pharisee (ch. xviii.).

We must place by itself another very remarkable and significant parable, related by St. Matthew in that part of his Gospel which seems to contain what have been called the special laws of the evangelical kingdom, such as the counsels of chastity, poverty, and obedience, humility, childlike temper, perfect for-

giveness of injuries, and the precept of fraternal correction.   The parable of which we speak is that of
the Labourers in the Vineyard—one which has given
more difficulty to commentators who have not understood its occasion and purport than perhaps any other.
And this leads us on to the last group of parabolic
instructions, which were delivered either to the Jews
in the Temple during the early days of Holy Week,
or to the Apostles on Mount Olivet, at the time when
the last great prophecy of the destruction of Jerusalem
and the end of the world had just been given.   They
are introduced by the parable of the Lord and his
Servants (St. Luke xix.), delivered as our Lord was
drawing nigh to Jerusalem, "because they thought
that the kingdom of God should immediately be
manifested."   The parables delivered to the Jews are
those, first, of the Two Sons (St. Matt. xxi.), already
alluded to, which was specially directed to the Chief
Priests and Scribes, the Wicked Husbandmen (St.
Matt. xxi., St. Mark xii., St. Luke xx.), and the
Marriage Supper (St. Matt. xxii.), where the incident
of the wedding garment is introduced.   Those delivered to the disciples are the parables of the Virgins
St. Matt. xxv.), the Talents (*ib.*), and—if that is
indeed to be considered a parable, and not rather a
simple prophecy—that of the Sentence of the Judge
on the merciful and the unmerciful (*ib.*).

The length of this rapid enumeration of the various
parts of this glorious and wonderful mass of doctrine
is enough to excuse us from the attempt of speaking
in detail on each of the parables of which it is composed, but we may find room in our present paper to

justify in regard of them the general view which we have taken of the subject of the parabolic teaching. The image of the Good Shepherd, like that of the Door, and those in later chapters of St. John, of the Grain of Corn (ch. xii.) and of the Vine (ch. xv.), do not need any explanation beyond that which is given by our Lord Himself, and their application is obvious. They picture in the most striking manner the love of God in the Incarnation, and their details contain many precious truths as to the economy of grace· The parable of the Good Samaritan, as we commonly call it, was spoken in answer to the famous question, "Who is my neighbour?" Touchingly beautiful as it is as a simple history, the interpretation which would be satisfied with supposing that an act of extraordinary charity on the part of a human way-farer is here set forth as our example cannot content us, as it has never contented the Fathers of the Church. No; the Person Whom we are called upon to imitate is our own great Father, God, in the In-carnation; the "man who fell among thieves" is a perfect theological picture of man wounded as he is by the Fall. We are thus taught that as our for-giveness to others is to be measured on the model of the forgiveness of God to us, so our charity to others is to be as close as possible an imitation of the great work of charity—the Incarnation. Thus the mind at once rises to the same great subject of God's dealings with us. So accurate is the picture that the theologians of the Church, in their teaching about the effects of the Fall, are often accustomed to draw arguments rather than mere illustrations

from the details of this parable. The work of mercy
which God has committed to us is a continuation of
the work of mercy begun by Him, and the whole
range of objects on which our mercy is to shed itself
forth for their relief is figured in the parable, because
the miseries of the wounded man represent accurately
the physical and moral miseries which have been
introduced into the world in consequence of the Fall,
which miseries it was the purpose of the Incarnation
to relieve, either directly or indirectly.

Again, God in His dealings with earnest prayer,
which He often refrains from granting for a while,
and then yields to importunity, is the subject of the
parable of the Friend roused up at midnight. God,
in His dealings with those who take to themselves
His gifts as their own property, and set their heart
upon riches, is the chief figure in the parable of the
Rich Fool ; for it is the forgetfulness of His Master-
ship, and of the suddenness with which He calls
men to account for their soul, which constitutes the
folly which is so soon brought to nought. God's
ways of dealing with His servants, the suddenness of
His coming, as if to try their fidelity, the immense
rewards which He is ready to bestow on the vigilant
—" He will gird Himself and make them sit down to
meat, and, passing by, will minister unto them ;" and
"Verily, I say to you, He will set him over all that
He possesseth ;"—and, on the other hand, the severe
but carefully-measured justice with which He will
punish negligence—these are the features added to
our theology by the parable about the servants.
God's providential patience with communities and

single persons, especially, of course, His patience
with the Jewish people, is the subject of the parable
of the Fig-tree. In that of the Narrow Gate (St.
Luke xiii.), which is not, however, formally a parable,
the same image is, to a certain extent, supplemented
by the description, which occupies almost the whole
passage, of the rejection of those who are not able
to enter in.* This is in reality a prophecy. The
parable, as it is called, about those invited to supper,
who are exhorted to take the lowest place, is at first
sight a puzzle on two accounts. The truth that is
set forth appears to be set forth without any image
at all, and the motive suggested for taking the lowest
place is not the noblest motive. But this, again, is
in reality a parable which sets forth the dealings and
the character of God, Who always exalts those who
humble themselves and humbles those who exalt
themselves. The same truth lies behind the parable
(which also may be a simple anecdote, and no figure)
of the Pharisee and the Publican (St. Luke xviii.),
as in that also which immediately precedes it, that of
the Unjust Judge, we have another repetition of the
truth that God is pleased to allow Himself to be

---

* "But when the Master of the House shall be gone in and shall
shut the door, you shall begin to stand without and knock at the door,
saying, Lord, open to us. And he answering shall say to you, I know
you not whence you are. Then you shall begin to say, We have eaten
and drunk in Thy presence, and Thou hast taught in our streets. And
He shall say to you, I know you not whence you are, depart from Me
all ye workers of iniquity. There shall be weeping and gnashing of
teeth, when you shall see Abraham and Isaac and Jacob and all the
prophets in the kingdom of God, and you yourselves thrown out"
(St. Luke xiii. 25—28).

done violence to by importunate prayer.   There is
no real comparison, of course, between the unjust
judge and God ; but our Lord argues *à fortiori*—
"And will not God revenge His elect, who cry to
Him day and night ? "*   We need hardly draw out
the teaching concerning God contained in such
parables as that of the Great Supper, of which it is
surely not an adequate account to say that it is
meant to illustrate the truth that men refuse the
offers of God on account of their love for earthly
goods.   The manner in which the supper is supplied
with guests, and the stern rejection of those who
have once refused, "I say unto you that not one of
those men that were invited shall taste of My
Supper," is a picture of that characteristic of God
celebrated by our Blessed Lady, *Esurientes implevit
bonis, et divites dimisit inanes,* of the principle which
has prevailed in His kingdom ever since the Angels
fell and men were called to fill their places.

Of this cycle of parables which we have mentioned as delivered chiefly in Judæa not long before
our Lord's last approach to Jerusalem, there remain
a few of the more celebrated to be illustrated by

* It should, however, be noted that there is something special in the
teaching here, which distinguishes it from such parables, for instance,
as that of the importunate friend at midnight.   The prayer here is distinctly for vengeance, and the passage should be compared to that
about the cry of the "souls under the altar of those that were slain for
the word of God, and for the testimony which they held" (Apoc. vi.
9—11).   This part of St. Luke's Gospel is probably drawn from mate-
rials collected by him while St. Paul was in prison at Cæsarea for two
years (Acts xxiv.), at a time when the Christians were groaning under
persecution.   This may help to explain v. 8.

what we suppose to be the general view and aim of
our Lord in His teaching of this kind. There are
the three great parables in the fifteenth chapter of
St. Luke, the combined meaning of which is too
obviously to our purpose to need more than simple
mention—the parable of the Lost Sheep, of the Lost
Piece of Silver, and of the Prodigal Son. The unity
of purpose in this wonderful chain of parables is
manifest from the ending of the last, if from nothing
else ; for at the beginning of the parable of the Lost
Sheep we are told of the murmuring of the Scribes
and Pharisees at our Lord's condescension to sinners
and at the end of the parable of the Prodigal we
have the picture of the elder brother, so exactly
answering to the conduct of those whose murmuring
gave occasion to the whole discourse. It is useful to
have so certain an instance of unity of purpose in
different parables, because we learn from this that it
is a characteristic of this mode of teaching that
various truths concerning the same subject are more
naturally told in different parables than in one, while,
at the same time, a parable may be made to develope,
as it were, a second part, the subject of which is to
illustrate a new truth. The three together give us a
complete history of God's action towards sinners in
tolerating them awhile, in not refusing them many
good things to which they have, in an improper
sense, a natural right, in letting the will of His creatures go its own way, in anxiously seeking them,
whether in His own Home, the Church, or outside
the fold, in welcoming them back, and making His
Angels rejoice with Him over their recovery. It shows,

if we may so say, how full our Lord's loving Heart was of the dealings of God to man, that He should have been at the pains to draw out so elaborately the full picture of those dealings on occasion of a simple murmuring against His own condescension, and it is remarkable how the strain of condescension is carried on even to the end, where the elder son is rebuked only in the gentlest way by the remonstrance and almost the apology of his father.

The two parables that follow—those, namely, of the Unjust Steward, in the sixteenth chapter of St. Luke, and of the Rich Glutton and Lazarus, in the same chapter—are of that secondary class in point of form of which we have already noticed some instances. There is no actual representation of one thing by another, nor is there any declaration that the kingdom of heaven is like this or that. Both of them might be true stories. But they are commonly reckoned among the parables, and belong to the same class of teaching with the rest. And here, too, we might contend that the principal object throughout is to set forth the dealings of God with man, instead of man's own way of acting. At this time of His teaching our Lord was particularly occupied in denouncing avarice and an undue love of earthly riches. The first parable, that of the Steward, teaches the true use of these riches; but the lesson is enforced by two truths which stand out from the narrative, the one that God will exact a strict account of the stewardship of every one; the other, that riches rightly used in alms-deeds are taken in satisfaction for sin, and purchase pardon. The same reference to the laws of God's kingdom concludes the story of the Rich Man and Lazarus, in which the veil that hides the unseen world is lifted up, and two great principles of the providential order are put forward in the words, first, "Remember that thou didst receive good things in thy lifetime, and likewise Lazarus evil things;" and then, "If they believe not Moses and the prophets, neither will they believe if one rise again from the dead"—which are full, moreover, of actual prophetic meaning.

The great parable of the Labourers in the Vineyard would require a long essay to itself to draw all its significance. We may, however, remark that its difficulties will vanish to a great extent if it is considered in the light of the context, and especially in the view which is here maintained that the laws of the Divine government of the world, and especially in the Church, form the main subject of the parabolic teaching. It was just after the memorable case of the rich young man who had come to our Lord to ask what he must do to gain eternal life, and had been offered the highest and noblest of vocations, " If thou wilt be perfect, go sell what thou hast and give to the poor, and thou shalt have treasure in heaven, and come, follow Me."* Just before, too, our Lord had set forth another counsel of perfection, that of absolute chastity, and had said pointedly, " All men take not this word, but they to whom it is given. He that can take, let him take it." And then St. Peter had asked his famous question, " Behold, we have left all things and followed Thee, what

* St. Matt. xix. 16, seq.

therefore shall we have ?" Our Lord first promised
to them the special reward of the Apostolical office,
and then added the hundred-fold and life everlasting
for all those who left what they had to leave for Him.
"And many that are first shall be last, and the last
first." The parable which follows is evidently a
commentary on these last words, which are repeated
at its close, after the answer of the householder to
the labourers who had entered first, and who had
complained of the reward given to the others. " Is it
not lawful for Me to do what I will ? Is thy eye evil,
because I am good ? So shall the first be last, and
the last first. For many are called, but few chosen."

These simple considerations go far towards explain-
ing the main drift of this parable. Our Lord's teaching
at this time, mainly addressed to His disciples only,
turned upon the difference of vocations in the kingdom of God. There are some to whom counsels of
perfection are addressed, some who cannot " take "
them. There are some who are not called to leave
all and follow Christ in the closest way, and some
who are called to that. St. Peter's question had
elicited from our Lord a declaration of the surpassing
reward which awaits those who have high vocations
and follow them faithfully. It may be said that the
whole system of formal states of perfection in the
Church is founded upon the doctrine here laid down.
That doctrine implies that God, Who is just and
bountiful to all, yet chooses whom He will for
the higher callings in His kingdom. He is the
Father of all, the Lover of all souls ; but there are
those whom He calls to higher privileges and more

glorious states in this world and in the next than others. But yet the masterful freedom of God in His choice and in the distribution of His gifts goes still further yet. The rewards of the next world do not necessarily correspond to the outward callings in this. There are first who are last, there are last who are first. Those who are called to states of perfection, or, again, to conspicuous positions in the visible Church, or to Apostolical labours and duties, are not of necessity either the only chosen ones of God or His dearest souls. Notwithstanding the preeminence of such states, the really highest places in heaven are for the saints, those who are truly nearest to God in this world and in the next; and the saints are to be found in all vocations and states of life—married or single, secular or religious, princes, warriors, as well as priests, rich as well as poor, young as well as old, not according to the quality of their outward state, but according to the intensity and richness of their inward grace and the faithfulness of their co-operation with it. God may put the highest graces in the lowest vocations, He may raise to consummate perfection in a few weeks or months as in a long course of years. This free munificence and absolute choice of God is the main lesson concerning Him in the parable before us. It is a law of His action, as truly as the law of exalting the humble and resisting the proud. To all He can say, " I do thee no wrong ;" I give thee what thou hast deserved and far more. " I will give unto this last even as unto thee. It is not lawful for Me to do what I will ? " Surely we may venture to say that

without this lesson the docrine as to counsels and
states of perfection would have been even incom-
plete. And the law of God's free choice in the dis-
posal of His gifts is the same, in whatever of its
operations we seek the more particular interpretation
of the details of the parable. We find no fault with
those who understand the callings at the several
hours of the historical dealings of God with the Jews
or Gentiles, for it is important to bear in mind the
truth that He acts towards nations and communities
as wholes, and in great measure on the same principle as with single persons. In any case, the Divine
law on which the parable turns is that expressed in
the words already quoted, " Is it not lawful for Me
to do what I like ? " Glory and reward always
correspond to grace and virtue ; but grace and virtue
are gifts of God, and they are not distributed by
Him in any servile obedience to the state or con-
dition in which His Providence has placed us. Nor
do we find fault with another usual interpretation,
according to which the envious selfishness of the
murmurers is the vice against which we are warned.
Rather it is clear from all history—from the history
of the conduct of the Chief Priests and Pharisees to
our Lord down to the most recent experience—that
no temptation is more dangerous to those who are
favoured by high vocations in God's external kingdom, as ecclesiastics, or dignitaries, or workers in
His vineyard, than the temptation to jealousy or
envy—the peculiar temptation of those whose states
secure them from grosser falls. Such faults are often
obvious to all but those who fall under them, as the
envious motives of our Lord's enemies were obvious

to the Roman Governor. "For he knew that for envy they had delivered Him."*

Another great doctrine about God is contained in the parable of the Lord and his servants, which may have been meant to steady the excited expectations of our Lord's followers as to some immediate external triumph, without serious long-continued conscientious work for their Master. It is another manifestation of the mastery and dominion of God that is contained both in the parable generally, and especially in the treatment of the negligent over-cautious servant, who thinks he does enough for his lord when he brings him back what he has received from him—"Lord, behold here is thy pound, which I have laid up in a napkin." Yes, there is a sense in which it is true of God—"Thou knewest that I was an austere man, taking up what I laid not down, and reaping that which I did not sow;" that is, He requires work and fruitfulness, the sweat of the brow and the toil of the brain, and the multiplied pounds—"His own 'with usury.'" But then it is He that gives the power as well as the occasion to work; it is He that guides the labouring hand and gives life and energy to the teeming brain. The multiplication of the pounds is His work, the success of the labour is His, and the reward of the labour is ours. "A necessity lieth upon me," says St. Paul,† "for woe is unto me if I preach not the Gospel!" And our Lord had already insisted upon this truth to the Apostles, when He had told them in one of those parables of the secondary kind, of which we have omitted special notice,‡ how men behave to their servants, even after they have

---

* St. Matt. xxvii. 18.   † I Cor. ix. 16.   ‡ St. Luke xvii. 7.

laboured all the day, making them when they return home first bring their masters' dinner and wait upon them, and not till after that take their own refreshment. " Doth he thank that servant for doing those things which he commanded him ? I think not. So you also, when you shall have done all those things that are commanded you, say, We are unprofitable servants, we have done that which we ought to do." So frequently does our Lord insist upon that entire dominion of God over us, which it is so easy and so pernicious to forget.

We thus come to the parables of the Holy Week. That of the Two Sons has already been spoken of.* That of the Vineyard and Husbandmen, which immediately follows, is applied by our Lord Himself to the fearful rejection and chastisement of the Jews for their continued abuse of God's graces, and it contains, moreover, the doctrine of God's long-continued patience and of the public vengeance with which He at last visits those who have persecuted His messengers—the guilt of which persecution, in the case of the Jews, was to be so awfully enhanced by their murder of His Son. And we must observe the force with which our Lord† insists on the Scriptural principle, " The stone which the builders rejected, the same is become the head of the corner "—quoting words which were afterwards used by St. Peter and St. Paul. In the same way the parable which stands next in order, the last which our Lord addressed to any but His own disciples—that of the Marriage

---

* St. Matt. xxi. 28—32.

† St. Matt. xxi. 42 ; St. Mark xii. 10, 11 ; St. Luke xx. 17, 18; *Vita Vitæ*, § 136.

Feast, is a picture of the law of divine action towards men. It repeats in a more pointed manner the lesson as to God's dealings contained in the former parable of the Great Supper, but it varies the details in a manner that gives it a prophetical reference to the same subject as the last. Here it is not merely, " I pray thee hold me excused," but they " laid hands on His servants, and having treated them contumeliously, put them to death. And when the King heard of it, He was angry, and sending His armies, He destroyed those murderers, and burnt their city."* Then, again, another parable is made to attach itself to the latter part of the original, that of the guest without a wedding garment. And here again we have another feature in the image of God as He reveals Himself in His dealings to us—His severe purity that will not allow anything unclean or common in His sight, and that jealous punishment of presumption which is as characteristic of Him as His immense mercifulness, condescension, and bounty.

Again, deeply significant as are the last of all the parables, those of the Ten Virgins, the Talents, and —if that be one—the image of the Last Judgment, with which the twenty-fifth chapter of St. Matthew concludes, the doctrine which they teach us about God is so unmistakeable as to make it unnecessary for us here to dwell upon them at any length. It is the suddenness with which He will call us to account, or the severity with which He will visit simple negligence, or again, the reward of those who are found ready, and the abundant recompense of those who have laboured faithfully, or the peculiar love with

* St. Matt. xxii. 6, 7.

which He regards works of mercy, which seem to be, in a sense, more dear to Him than the acts of other virtues for a particular reason connected with the great subject on which we have been all along engaged—that of His providential government of the world. For, let it be asked, as it often is asked, with misgivings and doubts, which, under the present state of society, have taken deep hold of many a heart that would willingly find no difficulty in the doctrine of Providence—let it be asked how has God—Who feeds the ravens who call upon Him, clothes the lilies of the field, and lets not a sparrow fall to the ground without His knowledge and permission—how has He provided for the numberless wants of those who are of more value than many sparrows, the hungry, the naked, the poor, orphans, widows, the sick, the afflicted of every class? The answer is surely this, that apart from special interpositions of His power, He has provided for them by the Christian charity of their brethren. He has left them to us, and He has made us the ministers charged with the execution of His behests of mercy to them, as He has charged earth and air and dew and rain and sea, the teeming ground, the fostering ray, the genial shower, fruits and trees and herbs and flowers, and all the resources of nature, to provide for the wants of His lower creatures. The machinery of nature does not fail—well would it be if our charity and mercy to our fellow-men failed as little!

Mercy, then, is the provision which God, the Author and Ruler of society, and especially of Christian society, has made for human miseries, manifold as they are; and this great scene of the Judgment Day

thus answers in a remarkable manner to the parable
of the Good Samaritan. Thus also it appropriately
closes the long series of the parables. We can see
how it is that in this great unfolding of the ways of
God to mankind in His providence, the closing scene
of the whole history should be made by our Blessed
Lord to turn upon the judgment of men as to this
point—how they have fulfilled their duty as to the
administration of that service of mercy which is their
peculiar part, a part which God has so much at heart,
in the great order of His kingdom. Doubtless He
repairs in a thousand ways the effects of their cold-
ness and negligence; doubtless He crowns a thousand virtues and punishes a thousand faults, beside
the virtue of mercy and the fault of unmercifulness.
But it is a law of His kingdom, a law set forth in
the Old Testament as well as in the New, that " He
gave to every one commandment concerning his
neighbour,"* and the first sin committed against
human society was that of him who asked, " Am I
my brother's keeper? "† No wonder, then, that the
last of our Lord's revelations concerning His Father
in publicly judging the world through Him, should
be that which tells us how strictly this law will be
vindicated, how much will depend on our practical
remembrance or practical forgetfulness of His own
most tender words—"Amen, I say to you, as long as
you did it to one of these My least brethren, ye did
it unto Me "—to Me, your Brother and your Re-
deemer, the Beginning and Author of your regenerate
supernatural life ; to Me, your God, your Governor,
your Provider and Preserver, Who have committed

* Ecclus. xvii. 12. † Gen. iv. 19.

to you so large a share of the Providence on which your brethren depend.

We may add a single word as to the general principle of the interpretation of the details of the parables, as distinct from the purpose which we may assign to each of setting forth some great law of God's action in the government of His kingdom. The examples which we possess of the interpretation of parables by our Blessed Lord Himself, in the case of the parable of the Sower and that of the Tares or Cockle, certainly seem to favour the belief that almost every feature of the comparisons by which divine truths are thus represented has its counterpart in reality. At the same time this principle might probably be urged too far. In the second of these two great parables, for instance, one portion is left by our Lord unapplied, for there is nothing in His explanation which corresponds to the servants who go to the Master of the Field, and ask Him how it comes that there is a mixture of bad seed with good, to whom He gives the significant answer, "Let both grow until the harvest." We need only observe, that we have been occupied for the present with the more important point of ascertaining some general principle which may enable us to look at once to the great truths which are the main subject of the parabolic teaching, and that when that is once established, if it can be established with any accuracy, it must of necessity furnish a most valuable key to unlock the difficulties of the details of the picture in each case, instead of in any way excluding the idea of their deep and varied significance.

The Parables of Our Lord,

ARRANGED FOR THE DAYS IN LENT AND ADAPTED TO
THE LENTEN GOSPELS.

By FATHER SALMERON.

—o—

ASH-WEDNESDAY. *Gospel* on the right dispositions for fasting.
—Matt. vi. 16—21.

Parable of the Sower who went out to sow
his seed.—Matt. xiii. 1—9.

THURSDAY ....*Gospel* on the faith of the Centurion surpassing that of the Israelites.—Matt. viii.
5—13.

Parable of the two sons sent by their father
into his vineyard.—Matt. xxi. 33—41.

FRIDAY ....*Gospel* on the love of our enemies and the
forgiveness of injuries.—Matt. v. 43 to
vi. 4.

Parable of the Unmerciful Servant.—Matt.
xviii. 23—35.

SATURDAY...........*Gospel* on the coming of our Lord to His
Apostles after the fourth watch, when
they had laboured all night against the
wind.—Matt. xiv. 47—56.

Parable of the Grain of Mustard-seed,
which, when bruised, becomes pungent,
as men are made perfect by tribulation.
—Matt. xiii. 31, 32.

E

FIRST SUNDAY IN LENT .... } *Gospel* on our Lord's Temptation.—Matt. iv. 1—11.

Parable on the strong armed man.—Luke xi. 21, 22.

MONDAY................*Gospel* on the coming of Christ to the Judgment, in which is the—

Parable of the Pastor with the goats and sheep.—Matt. xxv. 31—46.

TUESDAY ....*Gospel* on the expulsion of the buyers and sellers from the temple by our Lord after his entry into Jerusalem.—Matt. xxi. 10—17.

Parable of the Net which is cast into the sea and gathers into its meshes all sorts of fish.—Matt. xiii. 47—50.

WEDNESDAY.........*Gospel.*—Our Lord severely rebukes the Pharisees for tempting Him, and prefers the Ninevites to them.—Matt. xii. 38—50.

Parable of the Fig-tree which for three years brought not forth fruit.— Luke xiii. 6—9.

THURSDAY.............*Gospel.*—The importunity of the woman of Canaan with our Lord.—Matt. xv. 21—28.

Parable of the Unjust Judge.—Luke xviii. 2—8.

FRIDAY ....*Gospel.*—The paralytic at the pool, who is asked whether he would be made whole. —John v. 1—15.

Parable of the Seed growing silently.— Mark iv. 26—29.

SATURDAY, AND THE SECOND SUNDAY IN LENT .... } *Gospel* of the Transfiguration.—Matt. xvii. 1—9.

Parable of the Master who sends workmen into the vineyard and rewards them all alike with a penny.—Matt. xx. 1—16.

MONDAY...............*Gospel.*—" I go, and you shall seek me, and you shall die in your sin."—John viii. 21—29.

Parable.—" Let your loins be girt up and lamps burning in your hand, &c."— Luke xii. 35—37.

TUESDAY ....*Gospel* on the obedience due to the ordinations of the Scribes and Pharisees, according to whose doings we ought not to do.—Matt. xxiii. 1—12.

Parable.—" Who, thinkest thou, is a faithful and wise servant ? &c."—Matt. xxiv. 45—47.

WEDNESDAY.........*Gospel* on the petition of the two sons of Zebedee for the first seats in Heaven.— Matt. xx. 17—28.

Parable.—" When thou art invited to a wedding, sit not down in the first place, &c."—Luke xiv. 7—11.

THURSDAY............*Gospel* on Lazarus and the glutton.— Luke xvi. 19—31.

Parable of the Rich Man who knew not where to store away his plentiful crops.— Luke xii. 16—21.

FRIDAY ....*Gospel.*—The—

Parable of the Vineyard planted by the householder, hedged round, and furnished with a press and a tower, and let out to husbandmen, &c.—Matt. xxi. 33—46.

SATURDAY............*Gospel.*—The—

Parable of the Prodigal Son.—Luke xv. 11—32.

THIRD SUNDAY } *Gospel* contains the assertion of the Phari-
IN LENT......... } sees that our Lord cast out devils by
Beelzebub.—Luke xi. 14—28.

Parable.—The return of the unclean spirit,
with seven other spirits more wicked than
himself, to the house whence he came
out.—Luke xi. 24—26.

MONDAY.............*Gospel.*—Our Lord's complaint that He has
not found faith amongst the Nazarenes.—
Luke iv. 23—30.

Parable of the Leaven which a woman hid
in three measures of meal.—Luke xiii.
20, 21.

TUESDAY ....*Gospel* on the duty of fraternal correction.
—Matt. xviii. 15—22.

Parable of the Good Samaritan.—Luke x.
33—37.

WEDNESDAY.........*Gospel* contains the—

Parable.—" Not that which goeth into the
mouth defileth a man, &c."—Matt. xv.
10—20.

THURSDAY...........*Gospel.*—Our Lord heals St. Peter's mother-
in-law.—Luke iv. 38.—44.

Parable of the Friend who comes at midnight
to ask for three loaves.—Luke xi. 5—13.

FRIDAY ....*Gospel.*— Conversion of the Samaritan
woman.—John iv. 5—42.

Parable of the Shepherd seeking the lost
sheep.—Matt. xviii. 12—14.

SATURDAY...........*Gospel.*—The woman taken in adultery
and brought to our Lord. — John viii.
1—11.

Parable of the Groat, lost and found.—
Luke xv. 8—10.

FOURTH SUNDAY } *Gospel.*—The miraculous multiplication of
IN LENT......... } loaves.—John vi. 1—15.

> *Parable* of the Iniquitous Steward who cheated his master.—Luke xvi. 1—8.

MONDAY ....*Gospel* on the first expulsion of the buyers and sellers from the Temple.—John ii. 13—25.

> *Parable* of the enemy who came and oversowed cockle among the wheat.—Matt. xiii. 24—30.

TUESDAY ....*Gospel.*—"My doctrine is not Mine, but His that sent Me."—John vii. 14—31.

> *Parable.*—How the servant is treated on returning from the field where he was sowing, &c."—Luke xvii. 7—10.

WEDNESDAY.........*Gospel* of the man who had been blind from birth.—John ix. 1—38.

> *Parable.*—"The light of thy body is thy eye."—Matt. vi. 22, 23.

THURSDAY ....*Gospel.*—The widow of Nain.—Luke vii. 11—16.

> *Parable* of the Merchant seeking good pearls.—Matt. xiii. 45, 46.

FRIDAY .... *Gospel.*—The raising of Lazarus.—John xi. 1—45.

> *Parable* of the Treasure hidden in the field. Matt. xiii. 44.

SATURDAY...........*Gospel.*—"I am the light of the world : he that followeth Me walketh not in darkness."—John viii. 12—20.

> *Parable* of the Light which must be placed upon a candlestick.—Mark iv. 21, 22.

PASSION SUNDAY. *Gospel.*—"Which of you shall convince Me of sin? &c."—John viii. 46—59.

Parable.—"Be at agreement with thy adversary betimes, whilst thou art in the way with him, &c."—Matt. v. 25, 26.

MONDAY ....*Gospel.*—Our Lord threatens to depart from the Jews.—John vii. 32—39.

Parable of the Nobleman who went into a distant country to gain himself a kingdom.—Luke xix. 12—27.

TUESDAY ....*Gospel.*—Our Lord's brethren bid Him go up to Judæa for the festival.—John vii. 1—13.

Parable.—"Who does not enter the sheepfold by the door . . . . he is a thief, &c."—John x. 1—10.

WEDNESDAY.........*Gospel.*—The Jews ask our Lord, on the feast of the Dedication, "How long dost Thou hold our souls in suspense? &c." —John x. 22—38.

Parable of the Good Shepherd.—John x. 11—18.

THURSDAY............*Gospel* contains the—

Parable of the two Debtors : the one owed five hundred pence, the other fifty.— Luke vii. 41—43.

FRIDAY ....*Gospel.*—The assembly of the priests and Pharisees against Jesus.—John xi. 47—54.

Parable of those summoned to the wedding and unwilling to come.—Matt. xxii. 2—14.

SATURDAY AND } *Gospel.*—Our Lord's reception on entering
PALM SUNDAY... } Jerusalem.—John xii. 10—36.
   Parable of the Virgins.—Matt. xxv. 1—12.

MONDAY ....*Gospel.*—The supper in Bethany.—John
   xii. 1—9.
   Parable.—"A certain man made a great
   supper, and invited many, &c."—Luke
   xiv. 16—24.

TUESDAY .. ..The same parable of the Supper may be
   applied to the Blessed Eucharist, to
   produce the dispositions requisite for
   worthy Communion.

WEDNESDAY.........*Parable* of the Treasure hidden in the
   field may be considered again, and in
   reference to the treasures and fruits
   received by worthy communicants.—
   Matt. xiii. 44.

HOLY THURSDAY, } *Gospel.*—Passion.—John xiii. 1—15.
OR GOOD FRIDAY } *Parable.*—"Unless the grain of wheat
   falling into the ground die, itself re-
   maineth alone, &c."—John xii. 24, 25.

EASTER SUNDAY ...To explain the joy upon the Resurrection
   of our Lord may be adduced the fol-
   lowing
   Parable.—The woman forgets the pangs of
   childbirth for joy that a man is born into
   the world.—John xvi. 21.

EASTER MONDAY *Gospel.*—The disciples beg our Lord to
   stay with them, because it is towards
   evening, &c.—Luke xxiv. 13—35.
   Parable.—The man having a mind to build
   a tower (Luke xiv. 28—30) ; or
   The king about to make war upon another
   king.—*Ibid.*

Easter Tuesday. On which is generally closed the series of Lenten discourses, we may suitably take the following :—" Every scribe instructed in the kingdom of Heaven is like to a man that is a householder, who bringeth out of his treasure new things and old" (Matt. xiii. 52); or, "Every one that .... heareth My words and doth them ..... is like to a man building a house, who digged deep and laid the foundation upon a rock, &c."—Luke vi. 48, 49.

Wyman & Sons, Printers, Great Queen Street, London, W.C.